Love, all alike, no season knows, nor clime,
Nor hours, age, months, which are the rags of time.

John Donne

First published 1997
This edition © Robert Frederick Ltd. 2000
Old Orchard Street, Bath BA1 1JU, England

Editorial selections © Robert Frederick Ltd. All rights reserved.

Printed and bound in India

Embrace

*a collection of poetry and prose
in celebration of love*

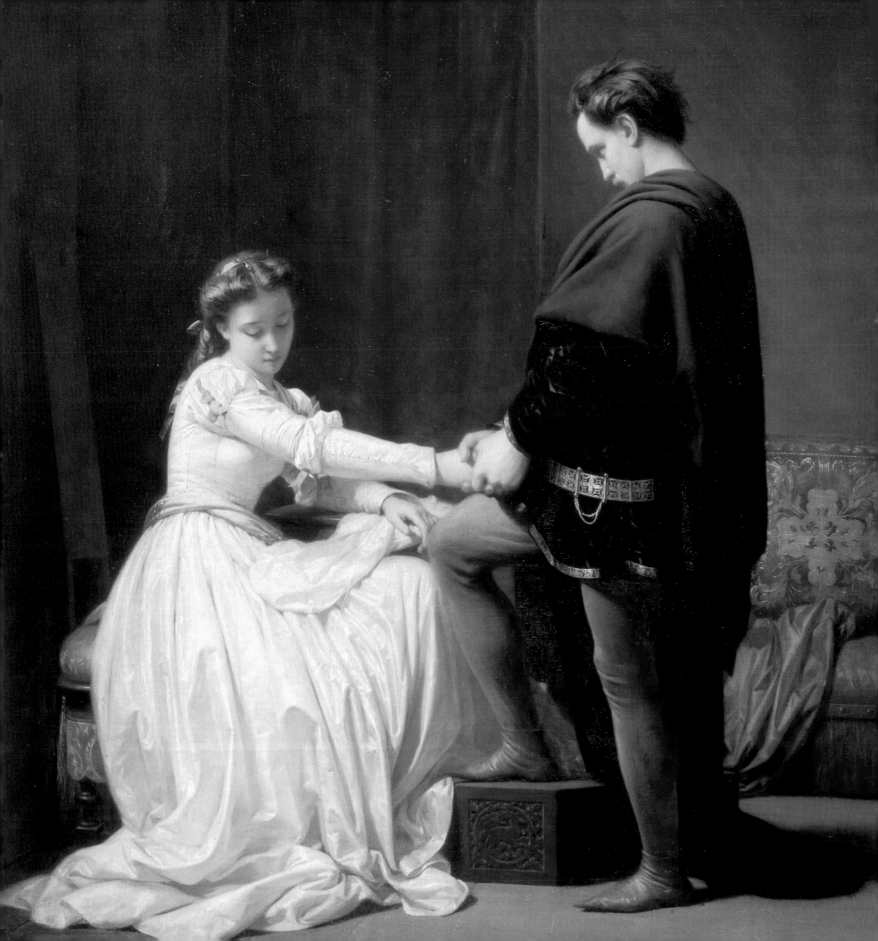

We are all born for love;
it is the principle of existence and its only end.

Benjamin Disraeli

frail like a flower

AESTAS

Who, being loved, is poor?

Oscar Wilde

And he went across to her and gathered her like a belonging in his arms. She was so tenderly beautiful, he could not bear to see her, he could only bear to hide her against himself. Now, washed all clean by her tears, she was new and frail like a flower just unfolded, a flower so new, so tender, so made perfect by inner light, that he could not bear to look at her, he must hide her against himself, cover his eyes against her. She had the perfect candour of creation, something translucent and simple, like a radiant shining flower that moment unfolded in primal blessedness. She was so new, so wonder-clear, so undimmed. And he was so old, so steeped in heavy memories. Her soul was new, undefined and glimmering with the unseen. And his soul was dark and gloomy, it had only one grain of living hope, like a grain of mustard seed. But this one living grain in him matched the perfect youth in her.

'I love you,' he whispered as he kissed her, and trembled with pure hope, like a man who is born again to a wonderful, lively hope far exceeding the bounds of death.

from Women in Love by D H Lawrence

Valentine:

And why not death, rather than living
    torment?
To die is to be banished from myself,
And Silvia is my self. Banished from her
Is self from self, a deadly banishment.
What light is light, if Silvia be not seen?
What joy is joy, if Silvia be not by—
Unless it be to think that she is by,
And feed upon the shadow of
    perfection.
Except I be by Silvia in the night
There is no music in the nightingale.
Unless I look on Silvia in the day
There is no day for me to look upon.
She is my essence, and I leave to be
If I be not by her fair influence
Fostered, illuminated, cherished,
    kept alive.
I fly not death to fly his deadly doom.
Tarry I here I but attend on death,
But fly I hence, I fly away from life.

from The Two Gentlemen of Verona
by William Shakespeare

Sonnet XLIII,
From The Portuguese

How do I love thee? Let me count the ways.
I love thee to the depth and breadth and height
My soul can reach, when feeling out of sight,
For the ends of Being and ideal Grace.
I love thee to the level of every day's
Most quiet need, by sun and candlelight.
I love thee freely, as men strive for Right;
I love thee purely, as they turn from Praise.
I love thee with the passion put to use
In my old griefs, and with my childhood's faith.
I love thee with a love I seemed to lose
With my lost saints, – I love thee with the breath,
Smiles, tears, of all my life! – and, if God choose,
I shall but love thee better after death.

Elizabeth Barrett Browning

'My great miseries in this world have been Heathcliff's miseries, and I watched and felt each from the beginning: my great thought in living is himself. If all else perished, and he remained, I should still continue to be; and if all else remained, and he were annihilated, the universe would turn to a mighty stranger: I should not seem a part of it. My love for Linton is like the foliage in the woods: time will change it, I'm well aware, as winter changes the trees. My love for Heathcliff resembles the eternal rocks beneath: a source of little visible delight, but necessary.

Nelly, I am Heathcliff! He's always, always in my mind: not as a pleasure, any more than I am always a pleasure to myself, but as my own being. So don't talk of our separation again: it is impracticable; and—'

She paused, and hid her face in the folds of my gown.

from Wuthering Heights by Emily Bronte

She was pale and trembling. He came to her relief with a fixed despair of himself which made the interview unlike any other that could have been holden.

'If it had been possible, Miss Manette, that you could have returned the love of the man you see before you—self-flung away, wasted drunken, poor creature of misuse as you know him to be—he would have been conscious this day and this hour, in spite of his happiness, that he would bring you to misery, bring you to sorrow and repentance, blight you, disgrace you, pull you down with him. I know very well that you can have no tenderness for me; I ask for none; I am even thankful that it cannot be. . . .

'I wish you to know that you have been the last dream of my soul. In my degradation I have not been so degraded but that the sight of you with your father, and of this home made such a home by you, has stirred old shadows that I thought had died out of me . . .

'. . . all through it, I have known myself to be quite undeserving. And yet I have had the weakness, and have still the weakness, to wish you to know with what a sudden mastery you kindled me, heap of ashes that I am, into fire—a fire, however, inseparable in its nature from myself, quickening nothing, lighting nothing, doing no service, idly burning away. . . .

'My last supplication of all, is this; and with it, I will relieve you of a visitor with whom I well know you have nothing in unison, and between whom and you there is an impassable space. It is useless to say it, I know, but it rises out of my soul. For you, and for any dear to you, I would do anything. If my career were of that better kind that there was any opportunity or capacity of sacrifice in it, I would embrace that sacrifice for you and for those dear to you. Try to hold me in your mind, at some quiet times, as ardent and sincere in this one thing. The time will come, the time will not be long in coming, when new ties will be formed about you—ties that will bind you yet more tenderly and strongly to the home you so adorn—the dearest ties that will ever

grace and gladden you. O Miss Manette, when the little picture of a happy father's face looks up in yours, when you see your own bright beauty springing up anew at your feet, think now and then that there is a man who would give his life to keep a life you love beside you!'

from A Tale of Two Cities by Charles Dickens

— 17 —

A kiss, when all is said, what is it?
An oath that's given closer than before;
A promise more precise; the sealing of
Confessions that till then were barely breathed;
A rosy dot placed on the *i* in loving;
A secret that is confined to a mouth and not to ears.

from Cyrano de Bergerac by Edmond Rostand

a promise more precise

He was not sure that he wanted to see the Countess Olenska again; but ever since he had looked at her from the path above the bay he had wanted, irrationally and indescribably, to see the place she was living in, and to follow the movements of her imagined figure as he watched the real one in the summerhouse. The longing was with him day and night, an incessant undefinable craving, like the sudden whim of a sick man for food and drink once tasted and long since forgotten. He could not see beyond the craving, or picture what it might lead to, for he was not conscious of any wish to speak to Madame Olenska or to hear her voice. He simply felt that if he could carry away the vision of the spot of earth she walked on, and the way the sky and sea enclosed it, the rest of the world might seem less empty.

from The Age of Innocence by Edith Wharton

One word
Frees us of all the weight
and pain of life:
That word is love.

Sophocles

They looked at each other at last, murmuring names that were a spell. Softly the two names lingered on the air, died away more slowly than other words, other names, slower than music in the mind.

'I don't know what came over me last night,' Rosemary said. 'That glass of champagne? I've never done anything like that before.'

'You simply said you loved me.'

'I do love you – I can't change that.' It was time for Rosemary to cry, so she cried a little in her handkerchief.

'I'm afraid I'm in love with you,' said Dick, 'and that's not the best thing that could happen.'

Again the names – then they lurched together as if the taxi had swung them. Her breasts crushed flat against him, her mouth was all new and warm, owned in common. They stopped thinking with an almost painful relief, stopped seeing; they only breathed and sought each other. They were both in the grey gentle world of a mild hangover of fatigue when the nerves relax in bunches like piano strings, and crackle suddenly like wicker chairs. Nerves so raw and tender must surely join other nerves, lips to lips, breast to breast. . . .

They were still in the happier stage of love. They were full of brave illusions about each other, tremendous illusions, so that the communion of self with self seemed to be on a plane where no other human relations mattered.

from Tender is the Night by F Scott Fitzgerald

Sometimes when one person is missing, the whole world seems depopulated.

Lamartine

tread

softly

I have spread my dreams under your feet:
Tread softly, because you tread on my dreams.

William Butler Yeats

Untitled

Bright star! would I were steadfast as thou art—
Not in lone splendour hung aloft the night
And watching, with eternal lids apart,
Like nature's patient, sleepless Eremite,
The moving waters at their priestlike task
Of pure ablution round earth's human shores,
Or gazing on the new soft fallen mask
Of snow upon the mountains and the moors—
No—yet still steadfast, still unchangeable,
Pillow'd upon my fair love's ripening breast,
To feel for ever its soft fall and swell,
Awake for ever in a sweet unrest,
Still, still to hear her tender-taken breath,
And so live ever—or else swoon to death.

John Keats

Beloved,–

I have not written to you for quite a long time: ah, I could not. I have nothing now to say! I think I could very easily die of this great happiness, so certainly do you love me! Just a breath more of it and I should be gone.

Good-bye, dearest, and good-bye, and good-bye! If you want letters from me now, you must ask for them! That the earth contains us both, and that we love each other, is about

my waking thought

all that I have mind enough to take in. I do not think I can love you more than I do: you are no longer my dream but my waking thought. I am waiting for no blue-moonrise now: my heart has not a wish which you do not fulfil. I owe you my whole life, and for any good to you must pay it out to the last farthing, and still feel myself your debtor.

Oh, Beloved, I am most poor and most rich when I think of your love; I can never let thought of you go!

Author Unidentified, from An English Woman's Love Letters, first published 1900

Ever has it been that love knows not its own depth until the hour of separation.

Kahlil Gibran

O, Were I Loved as I Desire to Be!

O, were I loved as I desire to be!
What is there in the great sphere of the earth,
Or range of evil between death and birth,
That I should fear,—if I were loved by thee?
All the inner, all the outer world of pain,
Clear love would pierce and cleave,
if thou wert mine;
As I have heard that somewhere in the main
Fresh-water springs come up through bitter brine.
'T were joy, not fear, clasped hand in hand
with thee,
To wait for death — must — careless of all ills,
Apart upon a mountain, though the surge
Of some new deluge from a thousand hills
Flung leagues of roaring foam into the gorge
Below us, as far on as eye could see.

Alfred Lord Tennyson

To feel, to touch your hand of love, full of sweet,
proud sensibilities . . . that hand polished
and soft with love, is a happiness as great as
your caress of honey and fire.

Honoré de Balzac to Countess Evelina Hanska

To leave is to die a little;
It is to die to what one loves.
One leaves behind a little of oneself
At any hour, any place.

Edmond Haraucourt

We two form a multitude.

Author Unidentified

Absence sharpens love; presence strengthens it.

Thomas Fuller

An Hour With Thee

An hour with thee! When earliest day
Dapples with gold the eastern grey,
Oh, what can frame my mind to bear
The toil and turmoil, cark and care,
New griefs, which coming hours unfold,
And sad remembrance of the old?
One hour with thee.

An hour with thee! When burning June
Waves his red flag at pitch of noon;
What shall repay the faithful swain,
His labour on the sultry plain;
And, more than cave or sheltering bough
Cool feverish blood and throbbing brow?
One hour with thee.

An hour with thee! When sun is set,
Oh, what can teach me to forget
The thankless labours of the day;
The hopes, the wishes, flung away;
The increasing wants, and lessening gains,
The master's pride, who scorns my pains?
One hour with thee.

Sir Walter Scott

one hour with thee

— 37 —

Maggie, I believe in you – I know you never meant to deceive me – I know you tried to keep faith to me, and to all. I believed this before I had any other evidence of it than your own nature. The night after I last parted from you I suffered torments. . . .

I will not tell you what I went through in that interval. But even in its utmost agony – even in those terrible throes that love must suffer before it can be disembodied of selfish desire – my love for you sufficed to withhold me from suicide, without the aid of any other motive. In the midst of my egoism, I yet could not bear to come like a death-shadow across the feast of your joy. I could not bear to foresake the world in which you still lived and might need me; it was part of the faith I had vowed to you – to wait and endure. Maggie, that is a proof of what I write now to assure you of – that no anguish I have had to bear on your account has been too heavy a price to pay for the new life into which I have entered in loving you. . . . You have been to my affections what light, what colour is to my eyes – what music is to the inward ear; you have raised a dim unrest into a vivid consciousness. . . . I even think sometimes that this gift of transferred life which has come to me in loving you, may be a new power to me.

I shall not go away. The place where you are is the one where my mind must live, wherever I might travel. And remember that I am unchangeably yours: yours – not with selfish wishes, but with a devotion that excludes such wishes.

God comfort you, my loving, large-souled Maggie. If everyone else has misconceived you, re-member that you have never been doubted by him whose heart recognized you ten years ago. . . .

Yours, to the last,

PHILIP WAKEM

from The Mill on the Floss by George Eliot

. . . for my sake, sweet, let the few years go by; we are married, and my arms are round you, and my face touches yours, and I am asking you, Were you not to me, in that dim beginning of 1846, a joy behind all joys, a life added to and transforming mine, the good I choose from all the possible gifts of God on this earth, for which I seemed to have lived . . . '

Robert Browning to Elizabeth Barrett

a joy behind all joys

Stolen Pleasure

My sweet did sweetly sleep,
And on her rosy face
Stood tears of pearl,
which beauty's self did weep;
I, wond'ring at her grace,
Did all amaz'd remain,
When Love said,
'Fool, can looks thy wishes crown?
Time past comes not again.'
Then did I me bow down,
And kissing her fair breast, lips,
cheeks, and eyes,
Prov'd here on earth the joys of paradise.

William Drummond of Hawthornden

Unable are the Loved to die
For Love is Immortality.

Emily Dickinson

The Evening Star

Lo! in the painted oriel of the West,
Whose panes the sunken sun incarnadines,
Like a fair lady at her casement, shines
The evening star, the star of love and rest!
And then anon she doth herself divest
Of all her radiant garments, and reclines
Behind the sombre screen of yonder pines,
With slumber and soft dreams
　　　of love oppressed.
O my beloved, my sweet Hesperus!
My morning and my evening star of love!
My best and gentlest lady! even thus,
As that fair planet in the sky above,
Dost thou retire unto thy rest at night,
And from thy darkened window
　　　fades the light.

Longfellow

From Doctor Faustus

Was this the face that launched
a thousand ships
And burnt the topless towers of Ilium?
Sweet Helen, make me immortal with a kiss.
Her lips suck forth my soul – see where it flies!
Come, Helen, come, give me my soul again.
Here will I dwell, for heaven is in these lips
And all is dross that is not Helena.
I will be Paris, and for love of thee
Instead of Troy shall Wittenberg be sack'd,
And I will combat with weak Menelaus,
And wear thy colours on my plumèd crest:
Yea, I will wound Achillis in the heel,
And then return to Helen for a kiss.
O thou art fairer that the evening air,
Clad in the beauty of a thousand stars!
Brighter art thou than flaming Jupiter,
When he appear'd to hapless Semele,
More lovely than the monarch of the sky
In wanton Arethusa's azur'd arms,
And none but thou shalt be my paramour!

Christopher Marlowe

make me immortal

On the contents of that letter depended all which this world could do for her! Anything was possible, anything might be defied, rather than suspense . . . and, sinking into the chair which he had occupied, succeeding to the very spot where he had leaned and written, her eyes devoured the following words:–

'I can listen no longer in silence. I must speak to you by such means as are within my reach. You pierce my soul. I am half-agony, half-hope. Tell me not that I am too late, that such precious feelings are gone for ever. I offer myself to you again with a heart even more your own than when you almost broke it, eight years and a half ago. Dare not say that man forgets sooner than woman, that his love has an earlier death. I have loved none but you. Unjust I may have been, weak and resentful I have been, but never inconstant. You alone have brought me to Bath. For you alone I think and plan. Have you not seen this? Can you fail to have understood my wishes? I had not waited even these ten days, could I have read your feelings, as I think you must have penetrated mine. I can hardly write. I am every instant hearing something which overpowers me. You sink your voice, but I can distinguish the tones of that voice, when they would be lost on others. Too good, too excellent creature! You do us justice, indeed. You do believe that there is true attachment and constancy among men. Believe it to be most fervent, most undeviating, in

'F.W.'

from Persuasion by Jane Austen

Alas! The love of women! it is known
To be a lovely and a fearful thing.

Lord Byron

Queen   Give me thy hand,
That I may dew it with my mournful tears;
Nor let the rain of heaven wet this place,
To wash away my woful monuments.
O, could this kiss be printed in thy hand,
That thou mightst think upon these by the seal,
Through whom a thousand sighs are breathed for thee!
So, get thee gone, that I may know my grief;
'Tis but surmised whiles thou art standing by,
As one that surfeits thinking on a want.
I will repeal thee, or, be well assured,
Adventure to be banished myself:
And banished I am, if but from thee.
Go; speak not to me; even now be gone.
O, go not yet! Even thus two friends condemn'd
Embrace and kiss and take ten thousand leaves,
Loather a hundred times to part than die.
Yet now farewell; and farewell life with thee!

Suffolk   Thus is poor Suffolk ten times banished;
Once by the king, and three times thrice by thee.
'Tis not the land I care for, wert thou thence;
A wilderness is populous enough,
So Suffolk had thy heavenly company:
For where thou art, there is the world itself,
With every several pleasure in the world,
And where thou art not, desolation.
I can no more: live thou to joy thy life;
Myself no joy in nought but that thou livest.

from The Second Part of King Henry VI by William Shakespeare

Sonnet

I wish I could remember that first day,
First hour, first moment of your meeting me,
If bright or dim the season, it might be
Summer or Winter for aught I can say;
So unrecorded did it slip away,
So blind was I to see and to foresee,
So dull to mark the budding of my tree
That would not blossom yet for many a May.
If only I could recollect it, such
A day o days! I let it come and go
As traceless as a thaw of bygone snow;
It seemed to mean so little, meant so much;
If only now I could recall that touch,
First touch of hand in hand –
Did one but know!

Christina Rossetti

Perfect love leaves no room for fear.

John, 1st Century

Hetty turned her head towards him, whispered, 'I thought you wouldn't come,' and slowly got courage to lift her eyes to him. That look was too much: he must have had eyes of Egyptian granite not to look too lovingly in return.

'You little frightened bird! Little tearful rose! Silly pet! You won't cry again, now I'm with you, will you?'

Ah, he doesn't know in the least what he is saying. This is not what he meant to say. His arm is stealing round the waist again; it is tightening its clasp; his lips are meeting those pouting child-lips, and for a long moment time has vanished. He may be a shepherd in Arcadia for aught he knows, he may be the first youth kissing the first maiden, he may be Eros himself, sipping the lips of Psyche—it is all one.

There was no speaking for minutes after. They walked along with beating hearts till they came within sight of the gate at the end of the wood. Then they looked at each other, not quite as they had looked before, for in their eyes there was the memory of a kiss.

the memory of a kiss

from Adam Bede by George Eliot

As Angels

Though seas and land
betwixt us both
Our faith and troth,
Like separated souls,
All time and space controls:
Above the highest sphere we meet,
Unseen, unknown;
and greet as angels greet.

Richard Lovelace

I am yours so much

Most Beloved,

I have been thinking, staring at this blank piece of paper, and wondering how there am I ever to say what I have in me here—not wishing to say anything at all, but just to be. I feel that I am living now only because you love me: and that my life will have run out, like this penful of ink, when that use in me is past. Not yet, Beloved, oh, not yet! Nothing is finished that we have to do and be:—hardly begun! I will not call even this 'midsummer,' however much it seems so: it is still only spring.

Every day your love binds me more deeply than I knew the day before: so that no day is the same now, but each one a little happier than the last. My own, you are my very own! And yet, true as that is, it is not so true as that I am your own. It is less absolute, I mean; and must be so, because I cannot very well take possession of anything when I am given over heart and soul out of my own possession: there isn't enough identity left in me, I am yours so much, so much!

Author Unidentified, from An English Woman's Love Letters,
first published 1900

I am going to America, and you to Italy.
The one or the other of us goes the wrong way, for the way will ever be wrong
which leads us further apart.

Thomas Jefferson to Maria Cosway

All who joy would win
Must share it, —
Happiness was born a Twin.

Lord Byron: Don Juan

My own Husband, – Let me call you so – I must – even if it makes you angry to think of such an unworthy wife as I. I must cry to you in my trouble – I have no one else! … I think I must die if you do not come soon, or tell me to come to you. … If you would come, I could die in your arms! I would be well content to do that if so be you had forgiven me!

Angel, I live entirely for you. … I am desolate without you, my darling, O, so desolate! I do not mind having to work: but if you will send me one little line, and say, 'I am coming soon,' I will bide on, Angel – O, so cheerfully! …

Have you never felt one little bit of what you used to feel when we were at the dairy? If you have, how can you keep away from me? I am the same woman, Angel, as you fell in love with; yes, the very same! – not the one you disliked but never saw. What was the past to me as soon as I met you? It was a dead thing altogether. I became another woman, filled full of new life from you. How could I be the early one? Why do you not see this? …

Think – think how it do hurt my heart not to see you ever – ever! Ah, if I could only make your dear heart ache one little minute of each day as mine does every day and all day long, it might lead you to show pity to your poor lonely one. …

The daylight has nothing to show me, since you are not here, and I don't like to see the rooks and starlings in the fields, because I grieve and grieve to miss you who used to see them with me. I long for only one thing in heaven or earth or under the earth, to meet you, my own dear! Come to me – come to me, and save me from what threatens me! –

from Tess of the d'Urbervilles by Thomas Hardy

Acknowledgements

Rosaline (Woman with Roses) by Hugh de Twenebroke Glazebrook (1855-1937), Christies Photo Library, London; The Proposal by Alfred W Elmore, Christie's Photo Library, London; La Belle Dame Sans Merci by Sir Frank Dicksee (1853-1928), City of Bristol Museum and Art Library/Bridgeman Art Library, London; Where Next? by Edward Frederick Brewtnall (1846-1902), Sotheby's Picture Library; A Meeting on the Bridge by Emile Claus (1849-1924), Sotheby's Picture Library; Venetian Ladies Listening to the Serenade by Frank Cadogan Cowper (1877-1958), Sotheby's Picture Library; Youth by Sir Lawrence Alma-Tadema (1836-1912), Sotheby's Picture Library; The Secret, 1958 by William Henry Fisk (1827-84), Roy Miles Gallery, 29 Bruton Street, London W1/Bridgeman Art Library, London; Shelley and Mary in St. Pancras Churchyard by William Powell Frith (1819-1909), Sotheby's Picture Library; The Painter's Honeymoon by Lord Frederick Leighton, Christie's Photo Library, London; The Love Letter by John William Godward (1861-1922), The Maas Gallery, London/Bridgeman Art Library, London; The Awakening of Love by Gustave Schmatz Herbert, Christies Photo Library, London; The Poets Theme by John Callcott Horsley (1817-1903), Sotheby's Picture Library; The Minstrel's Lady by George Sheridan Knowles (1863-1931), Sotheby's Picture Library; The Prince's Choice by Thomas Reynolds Lamont (1826-1898), Sotheby's Picture Library; The Accolade by Edmund Blair Leighton (1853-1922), Christie's, London/Bridgeman Art Library, London; 'God Speed' by Edmund Blair Leighton (1853-1922), Christie's Photo Library, London; The Riven Shield by Philip Richard Morris (1838-1902), Roy Miles Gallery, 29 Bruton Street, London W1/Bridgeman Art Library, London; Hesperus by Sir Joseph Noel Paton (1821-1901), Glasgow Art Gallery and Musuem/Bridgeman Art Library, London; Romeo and Juliet by Henri Pierre Picou (1824-1895), Sotheby's Picture Library; Bitomart and Amoret, 1898, by Mary F Raphael (fl. 1889-1902), Sotheby's Picture Library; Summer by Sir William Ernest Reynold-Stephens (1862-1943), Whitford & Hughes, London/Bridgeman Art Library, London; The Wedding of St. George and Princess Sabre by Dante Gabriel Rossetti (1828-82), Tate Gallery, London/Bridgeman Art Library, London; Simpletons, The Sweet River by Sir Samuel Luke Fildes (1843-1927), Sotheby's Picture Library; The Boating Party by Gaston La Touche (1854-1913), Sotheby's Picture Library; La Belle Dame Sans Merci, 1893 by John William Waterhouse (1849-1917), Hessisches Landesmuseum, Darmstadt/Bridgeman Art Library, London; Saint Cecilia by John William Waterhouse (1849-1917), Private Collection/Fine Art Photographs; Miranda – The Tempest by John William Waterhouse (1849-1917), Sotheby's Picture Library; Venus and Adonis by Signey Harold Meteyard (1868-1947), Sotheby's Picture Library; The Huguenot by Sir John Everett Millais (1829-1896), Sotheby's Picture Library; The Siren by John William Waterhouse (1849-1915), Sotheby's Picture Library; The Year's at Spring, All's right with the World by Sir Lawrence Alma-Tadema (1836-1912), Sotheby's Picture Library; The Siren by John William Waterhouse (1849-1915), Sotheby's Picture Library; L'Innocence by William-Adolphe Bouguereau (1825-1905), Christies, London/Bridgeman Art Library, London
Other images © Robert Frederick Ltd. 1996